THE HISTORY OF THE CROSS

THE HISTORY
OF THE
CROSS

Norman Laliberte

and

Edward N. West

THE MACMILLAN COMPANY

NEW YORK 1960

First Printing
Library of Congress catalog card number: 59–8171

The Macmillan Company, New York
Brett-Macmillan Ltd., Galt, Ontario

PRINTED IN HOLLAND BY SMEETS LITHOGRAPHERS
UNDER THE SUPERVISION OF CHANTICLEER PRESS, INC.

INTRODUCTORY ESSAY

THE CROSS IS ONE OF THE MOST ANCIENT AND GENERALLY used religious symbols. It has been used in some form by almost all religions save those which are specifically opposed to symbolism or, as the case is with Islam, specifically opposed to the outstanding religion of the Cross, Christianity. Christianity, because of the manner of its Lord's death, came immediately to regard the Cross as the very symbol of man's redemption. When St. Paul asserts that his only glory is in the Cross of the Lord Jesus Christ,(1) he is stating something fundamental to the Christian religion. St. John had seen in the Cross the first step in the "lifting up" which would ultimately draw all men to the Lord Jesus.(2) It should be noted that St. John did not think of the Cross as something which, if borne with patience here, would result in the gift of a crown to take its place in the hereafter. Rather, he thought of the Cross as that which itself became the crown. This obviously mystical approach to the Cross is sound religion, but it is an idea incapable of iconographic representation. It should be noted, however, that no one in the first century was remotely interested in iconographic representation; the ordinary Jewish interpretation of the Second Commandment—that against graven images—was still too completely part of the Christian background.

Ordinary Jewish practice of the first century did, however, allow for the tracing of the sacred letter *Yod* in the thongs which bound the phylactery to the hand. (The phylactery was a small case containing the text prescribed in Deuteronomy(3) for binding on the hand and on the forehead—literally, between the eyes.) *Yod* was the first letter of God's sacred name in Hebrew. It was therefore with ease that Christians of Jewish background could adopt the use of the Chi (**X**), the first letter of the title Christ in Greek. That this letter **X** should also be the form of a familiar version of the cross—known technically as the *crux decussata*—made it inevitable that the signing in "his Name" should become identical with the signing of the Cross.

St. Ignatius of Antioch, who died in the year 107, is credited by the Orthodox Church with having originated the popular usage of signing oneself,(4) and indeed everything else, with the Sign of the Cross. Tertullian (A.D. 145–220), in his *De Corona,* says: "At every forward step and movement, at every going in and out, when we put on our clothes and shoes, when we bathe, when we sit at table, when we light the lamps, on couch, on seat, in all the ordinary actions of daily life, we trace upon the forehead the sign."(5) And Hippolytus says: "In all the ordinary occasions of life we furrow our foreheads with the sign of the Cross, in which we glory none the less because it is regarded as our shame by the heathen in presence of whom it is a profession of our faith."(6) This practice is of great significance, since it will be used by the later Fathers as an argument against the wearing of any form of amulet—even including an *encolpion* (case) containing pages of the Gospels.(7)

In systematic argument with the Jews and with the pagan world, the Fathers indulged in a form of typology very difficult for the modern mind to follow. Justin Martyr (A.D. 114-165), in his *Dialogue with Trypho, a Jew,* declares that Christ's crucifixion and return in glory was symbolized both by the "tree of life, which was said to have been planted in paradise, and by those events which should happen to all the just." The rod which Moses used to divide the sea, bring water forth from the rock, and sweeten the bitter waters of Marah, was a type of the cross. The rods which Jacob placed in the water troughs, and with which he crossed the river, are types of the cross. The ladder of the heavenly vision and the stone he set up both symbolically proclaim Christ. Aaron's rod, the rod from the root of Jesse, the tree planted by the waterside, the palm tree like to which the righteous flourish, the tree from which God appeared to Abraham, the seventy willows which the people found after crossing Jordan, the rod and the staff of the Good Shepherd Psalm, the stick which Elisha cast into the Jordan—all these are types of the cross.(8) The whole passage is characteristic of the Church's argument with her ancient mother, Israel.

In dealing with pagans, the Church either appealed to those examples of pagan mythology or practice which she found commendable, or else attacked bitterly those which she found indefensible. Minucius Felix, writing in the year 166, says: "Crosses, moreover, we neither worship nor wish for. You, indeed, who consecrate gods of wood, adore wooden crosses perhaps as parts of your gods. For your very standards, as well as your banners, and flags of your camp, what else are they but crosses gilded and adorned? Your victorious trophies not only imitate the appearance of a simple cross, but also that of a man affixed to it. We assuredly see the sign of a cross, naturally, in the ship when it is carried along with swelling sails, when it glides forward with expanded oars; and when the military yoke is lifted up, it is the sign of a cross; and when a man adores God with a pure mind, with hands outstretched. Thus the sign of the cross either is sustained by a natural reason, or your own religion is formed with respect to it."(9) And Tertullian, in *Ad Nationes,* could write: "As for him who affirms that we are 'the priesthood of a cross,' we shall claim him as our co-religionist. A cross is, in its material, a sign of wood; amongst yourselves also the object of worship is a wooden figure. Only, whilst with you the figure is a human one, with us the wood is its own figure. Never mind for the present what is the shape, provided the material is the same: the form, too, is of no importance, if so be it be the actual body of a god. If, however, there arises a question of difference on this point, what (let me ask) is the difference between the Athenian Pallas, or the Pharian Ceres, and wood formed into a cross, when each is represented by a rough stock, without form, and by the merest rudiment of a statue of unformed wood? Every piece of timber which is fixed on the ground in an erect position is a part of a cross, and indeed the greater portion of its mass. But an entire cross is attributed to us, with its transverse beam, of course, and its projecting seat. Now you have the less to excuse you, for you dedicate to religion only a mutilated imperfect piece of wood, while others consecrate to the sacred purpose, a complete structure. The truth, however, after all, is that your religion is *all cross,* as I shall show. You are indeed unaware that your gods in their origin have proceeded from this hated cross."(10)

There is a famous graffito drawing in Rome, one which dates back to ancient days. This portrays an ass crucified, and inscribed beside it is the taunting legend, "Alexamenos worships his god."*(11)* Tertullian touches on this libel in a passage in *The Apology:* "For, like some others, you are under the delusion that our god is an ass's head. Cornelius Tacitus first put this notion into people's minds. In the fifth book of his histories, beginning the (narrative of the) Jewish war with an account of the origin of the nation; and theorizing at his pleasure about the origin, as well as the name and the religion of the Jews, he states that having been delivered, or rather, in his opinion, expelled from Egypt, in crossing the vast plains of Arabia, where water is so scanty, they were in extremity from thirst; but taking the guidance of the wild asses, which it was thought might be seeking water after feeding, they discovered a fountain, and thereupon in their gratitude they consecrated a head of this species of animal. And as Christianity is nearly allied to Judaism, from this, I suppose, it was taken for granted that we too are devoted to the worship of the same image. But lately a new edition of our god has been given to the world in that great city: it originated with a certain vile man who was wont to hire himself out to cheat the wild beasts, and who exhibited a picture with this inscription: The God of the Christians, born of an ass. He had the ears of an ass, was hoofed in one foot, carried a book, and wore a toga."*(12)*

In spite of libel, misunderstanding, betrayal, and persecution, the Church not only survived, but triumphed throughout the Roman Empire. The immediate agent of this triumph was the emperor Constantine. The earliest account of Constantine's conversion is written by Lactantius (A.D. 260–330). He writes: "Constantine was directed in a dream to cause *the heavenly sign* to be delineated on the shields of his soldiers, and so to proceed to battle. He did as he had been commanded, and he marked on their shields the letter X, with a perpendicular line drawn through it and turned round thus (P) at the top, being the cipher of CHRIST. Having this sign, his troops stood to arms."*(13)* Eusebius, in a later account, reports that Constantine, toward the end of his life, insisted that he had seen this sign in the heavens, rather than dreamed of it.*(14)* Most scholars accept this possibility, since there is a well-known natural phenomenon which would have an almost identical appearance with the figure described by Lactantius. In common with the strong east wind, which moved the waters of the

Red Sea so that the children of Israel could cross over, the problem for thoughtful people is not this natural phenomenon, but rather whether so critical and timely an agent of deliverance can be dismissed as "coincidence."

The emperor abolished crucifixion throughout the empire out of reverence for the Crucified One, and the Sacred Monogram, whether in X form or in the increasingly more popular cross form, became the honored public symbol of Christ.

In the fourth century a remarkable change came over the thinking and practice of the Church. This was vastly augmented by the terrible interlude under Julian the Apostate, who was killed in 363. Whereas Eusebius makes no mention of the Empress Helena, Constantine's mother, having had any connection with the True Cross, Cyril of Jerusalem, writing in the year 348, says that "the whole world has . . . since been filled with pieces of the wood of the Cross."*(15)* Sulpitius Severus (A.D. 363–420), writing a half-century later, gives details of the empress's discovery of the Cross.*(16)* Socrates Scholasticus (A.D. 379 to after 439), writing a century later, not only gives the details of her discovery of the Cross, but also of her building the Church of the New Jerusalem and leaving in it a portion of the Cross, enclosed in a silver case, and sending the other part to the emperor, who, in turn, privately enclosed it in his own statue for the protection of the city and empire.*(17)* Theodoret (A.D. 393–458), writing a few years after this, gives even more detail.*(18)*

Holy Cross Day, the Feast of the Exaltation (or Elevation) of the Precious Cross of the Lord, marks not only the dedication festival of the basilicas erected by Constantine on the sites of Calvary and the Holy Sepulchre but also of the Vision of Constantine, the Exaltation of the Relic at Jerusalem, and its triumphal return to Jerusalem in 628, after fourteen years in the hands of the Persian king.*(19)* The Gallican churches had a feast marking the Invention (the word actually means *discovery*) of the True Cross on May 3rd. (There is a lengthy and highly unedifying medieval legend about this discovery which need not concern us here.) The Feast of the Exaltation, in some form, dates back to the end of the fourth century, the Feast of the Invention to the seventh century. As so often happens in liturgical duplications, the Western Church has come to keep both days. It is interesting to note that one of the greatest of the Fathers, St. Gregory of Nyssa (A.D. 335–395?), treated the wood as a "sacramental." He writes: "And the wood of the Cross is of saving efficacy for all men, though it is, as I am informed, a piece of a poor tree, less valuable than most trees are. So a bramble bush showed to Moses the manifestation of the presence of God: so the remains of Elisha raised a dead man to life; so clay gave sight to him that was blind from the womb. And all these things, though they were matter without soul or sense, were made the means for the performance of the great marvels wrought by them, when they received the power of God."(20)

St. John Chrysostom (A.D. 347?–407) is fully aware of the tradition, since, in one of his *Homilies on St. John,* he notes that the Lord's Cross was recognized, first, by its lying in the middle, and then by its title, since those of the thieves had no titles.(21) In this connection, there is an oft-quoted passage of Paulinus of Nola which intimates to Sulpitius Severus that, though bits were frequently taken from the piece of the True Cross at Jerusalem, it grew no smaller. Before using or misusing such a quotation, it is wise to remember that the ancient Fathers rarely intended their words in an exclusively literal fashion.

Art, at the service of Religion, had, in the meantime, been making cautious attempts toward some adequate symbolic representation of Christ. The popular form was a T-shaped cross, with the representation of a lamb above it.(22) This conveyed, in purely symbolic terms, the Church's theology, but it left the hearts of picture-minded people woefully unsatisfied. It was with this in mind that the Council in Trullo (A.D. 692) passed the following Canon LXXXII: "In some pictures of the venerable icons, a lamb is painted to which the Precursor points his finger, which is received as a type of grace, indicating beforehand through the Law, our true Lamb, Christ our God. Embracing therefore the ancient types and shadows as symbols of the truth, and patterns given to the Church, we prefer 'grace and truth,' receiving it as the fulfillment of the Law. In order therefore that 'that which is perfect' may be delineated to the eyes of all, at least in coloured expression, we decree that the figure in human form of the Lamb who taketh away the sin of the world, Christ our God, be henceforth exhibited in images, instead of the ancient lamb, so that all may understand by means of it the depths of the humiliation of the Word of God, and that we may recall to our memory his conversation in the flesh, his passion and salutary death, and his redemption which was wrought for the whole world."(23)

The first pictorial representations of Christ on the Cross took for granted a legend contained in *The Gospel of Nicodemus,* a document which has been dated as anywhere from the third to the fifth centuries. The references to the Blessed Virgin in this writing would seem to indicate that the manuscript was either late fourth or early fifth century. The pertinent section reads: "Then they stripped Jesus, and the soldiers took his garments, and divided them among themselves; and they put on him a tattered robe of scarlet, and raised him, and drew him up on the cross at the sixth hour of the day."(24) The oldest known example is in a Syriac manuscript dated A.D. 586.(25) The Lord is shown as robed in a purple tunic reaching to the ankles. This form became so standard that there were riots in France at the first attempt to introduce the figure of the Lord unclothed.(26)

The Western Church's gradual essay into "realism" in art was not totally successful. In the first place, the first portrayals of the Crucifixion rarely had any nails shown, and it is to be noted that the crucifix in the Catacomb of Pope Julius follows the Gospel account strictly and has no sign of nails in the feet. (It is from Psalms that we derive the tradition of Christ's feet being pierced; the Gospels only mention wounds in the hands and in the side.)(27) In the second place, by the time "realism" came in, men had largely forgotten what crucifixion was like, save for a notion that crosses were T-shaped.(28) Actually crucifixion, as was indicated by Tertullian,(29) was done on a cross made up of three pieces: an upright, known as *stipes,* which was fixed in the ground; a transverse beam, known as *patibulum;* and a projecting seat to take the weight of the body and to produce increased tension on the thigh bones when the knees were drawn together under this saddle. This seat has largely been ignored by artists, and a foot rest, or *suppedaneum,* has been substituted for it. Socrates Scholasticus notes that the inscription which Pilate had written for Christ was on a board.(30) The inclusion of some form of extension to take this inscription accounts for the Latin cross. The nails in the hands were put there not only for the purpose of shattering the nervous system but also to make it possible for the person crucified to live longer. The principal agony of crucifixion was induced by the rigidity and strangulation caused by ropes.(31) The portion of the cross carried by the condemned was the crossbeam—the *patibulum*. The memory of this is still clear in *The Gospel of Nicodemus*.(32) One has only to be acquainted with these sickening details to realize how far short of realism "realistic" art has fallen.

This brief essay will have furnished the basic facts which must be considered in any thoughtful study of the Cross, but it will, of necessity, have done little to convey the splendid devotions which have surrounded it. On top of its natural and perfectly understandable attraction, there has been added the passionate loyalty of Christians who, during the Iconoclastic Controversy,(33) had been deprived of any other public symbol of their religion. Possibly the most moving summary of the Church's official attitude is that of St. John of Damascus in his Exposition of the Orthodox Faith: "Moreover, we worship even the image of the precious and life-giving Cross, although made of another tree, not honouring the tree (God forbid) but the image as a symbol of Christ. For he said to his disciples, admonishing them, *Then shall appear the sign of the Son of Man in Heaven,* meaning the Cross. And so also the angel of the resurrection said to the woman, *Ye seek Jesus of Nazareth which was crucified.* And the Apostle said, *We preach Christ crucified.* For there are many Christs and many Jesuses, but one crucified. He does not say speared but crucified. It behooves us, then, to worship the sign of Christ. For wherever the sign may be, there also will he be. But it does not behoove us to worship the material of which the image of the Cross is composed, even though it be gold or precious stones, after it is destroyed, if that should happen. Everything, therefore, that is dedicated to God we worship, conferring the adoration on him.

"The tree of life which was planted by God in Paradise pre-figured this precious Cross. For since death was by a tree, it was fitting that life and resurrection should be bestowed by a tree. Jacob, when he worshipped the top of Joseph's staff, was the first to image the Cross, and when he blessed his sons with crossed hands he made most clearly the sign of the cross. Likewise also did Moses' rod, when it smote the sea in the figure of the cross and saved Israel, while it overwhelmed Pharaoh in the depths; likewise also the hands stretched out crosswise and routing Amalek; and the bitter water made sweet by a tree, and the rock rent and pouring forth streams of water, and the rod that meant for Aaron the dignity of the high priesthood: and the serpent lifted in triumph on a tree as though it were dead, the tree bringing salvation to those who in faith saw their enemy dead, just as Christ was nailed to the tree in the flesh of sin which yet knew no sin. The mighty Moses cried, *You will see your life hanging on the tree before your eyes,* and Isaiah likewise, *I have spread out my hands all the day unto a faithless and rebellious people.* But may we who worship this obtain a part in Christ the crucified. Amen."*(34)*

The richness of liturgical devotion which the Cross has called forth may be observed in the following extracts from the Eastern Church's Special Service for the Feast of the Elevation of the Precious Cross of the Lord:*(35)*

> The Cross being set up, doth command every created being to sing the most pure Passion of him who was lifted up thereon. For having upon the same slain him who had slain us, he endowed with life those who were slain, and adorned them, and vouchsafed that they might dwell in heaven forasmuch as he is compassionate, through the rich abundance of his goodness. Wherefore, rejoicing, let us exalt his Name, and magnify his exceeding condescension.

> O come, all ye nations, let us adore the blessed Tree, through which the righteousness eternal hath come to pass: for he who beguiled our forefather Adam with the tree is himself beguiled by the Cross, and he who, like a tyrant, did lord it over that which the King had fashioned, falleth, being overthrown by a downfall strange. The poison of the serpent is washed away by the blood of God, and the curse of just condemnation is abolished, in that the Righteous One hath been condemned by unrighteous judgment; for it was meet that the tree should be healed by the Tree, and that by the passion of the Passionless One upon the Tree, the passions of the condemned one should be destroyed. But glory, O Christ our King, unto thy wise providence to usward, whereby thou hast saved all men, forasmuch as thou art good and lovest mankind.

Today is the Master of creation and Lord of glory nailed upon the Cross, and is pierced in the side, and of gall and vinegar doth the Sweetness of the Church partake. With a crown of thorns is he invested who covereth the heavens with clouds, and with the robe of scorn is he endued; and he who with his hand did fashion man is smitten by a human hand. He who clotheth the heavens with clouds is beaten upon his shoulders, and receiveth spitting and wounds, indignities and buffetings in the face; and he, my Redeemer and my Saviour, doth endure all these things for the sake of me, the accursed, that he may save the world from guile, forasmuch as he is compassionate.

The terse beauty of Latin devotion is seen in the following Collect for the same Feast:*(36)*

Deus, qui hodierna die Exaltationis sanctae Crucis annua solemnitate laetificas: praesta quaesumus; ut, cujus mysterium in terra cognovimus, ejus redemptionis praemia in coelo mereamur.	O God, who makest us glad this day by the yearly solemnity of the Exaltation of the Holy Cross: Grant, we beseech thee, that we who on earth have learned the mystery of our redemption, may be found worthy of its rewards in heaven.

The splendor of Latin hymnody on the subject may be seen in the following examples:*(37)*

Crux fidelis inter omnes
  Arbor una nobilis:
Nulla silva talem profert
  Fronde, flore, germine.
Dulce lignum, dulces clavos,
  Dulce ponde sustinet.
	Faithful Cross, above all other,
	  One and only noble tree!
	None in foliage, none in blossom,
	  None in fruit thy peer may be.
	Sweetest wood and sweetest iron,
	  Sweetest weight is hung on thee.

*   *   *   *

Arbor decora, et fulgida, Ornata Regis purpura, Electa digno stipite Tam sancta membra tangere.	O tree of beauty! tree of light! O tree with royal purple dight! What glory may with thine compare, Ordain'd those sacred limbs to bear!
O Crux ave, spes unica, Hoc Passionis tempore: Piis adauge gratiam, Reisque dele crimina.	O Cross, our sole reliance, hail! This holy passiontide avail, To win the just increase of grace And every sinner's crimes efface.

One of the most deeply beloved anthems of the Anglican Communion is a translation of the ancient Sarum anthem used in the Office of Unction:*(38)*

Salvator mundi salva nos, qui per crucem et sanguinem redemisti nos: auxiliare nobis te deprecamur Deus noster.

O Saviour of the world, who by thy Cross and precious Blood hast redeemed us; Save us, and help us, we humbly beseech thee, O Lord.

There is a touching and little-known hymn of Savonarola which concludes with this stanza:*(39)*

Jesus, may our hearts be burning
    With more fervent love for thee;
May our eyes be ever turning
    To thy Cross of agony;
Till in glory, parted never
    From the blessed Saviour's side,
Graven in our hearts for ever,
    Dwell the Cross, the Crucified.

Lutheran mysticism and devotion are beautifully summed up in this hymn of Johann Heermann:*(40)*

Thy blest Cross hath power to heal
    All the wounds of sin and strife.
Lost in thee, my heart doth feel
    Sudden warmth and nobler life.
In my saddest, darkest grief,
Let thy sweetness bring relief,
Thou who camest but to save,
Thou who fearest not the grave!

Free-Church piety has produced one of the best-loved hymns of the Cross:*(41)*

When I survey the wondrous cross
    Where the young Prince of Glory died,
My richest gain I count but loss,
    And pour contempt on all my pride.

Forbid it, Lord, that I should boast,
  Save in the cross of Christ, my God:
All the vain things that charm me most,
  I sacrifice them to his blood.

See, from his head, his hands, his feet,
  Sorrow and love flow mingled down!
Did e'er such love and sorrow meet,
  Or thorns compose so rich a crown?

Were the whole realm of nature mine,
  That were an offering far too small;
Love so amazing, so divine,
  Demands my soul, my life, my all.

A nineteenth century Anglican hymn speaks for both Apostolic and Patristic devotion to the Cross:(42)

In the cross of Christ I glory,
  Towering o'er the wrecks of time;
All the light of sacred story
  Gathers round its head sublime.

When the woes of life o'ertake me,
  Hopes deceive, and fears annoy,
Never shall the cross forsake me:
  Lo, it glows with peace and joy.

When the sun of bliss is beaming
  Light and love upon my way,
From the cross the radiance streaming
  Adds new luster to the day.

Bane and blessing, pain and pleasure,
  By the cross are sanctified;
Peace is there that knows no measure,
  Joys that through all time abide.

An Irish Evangelical hymn of the nineteenth century reads almost like a metrical version of a homily by St. John Chrysostom:(43)

> The Cross! It takes our guilt away;
>   It holds the fainting spirit up;
> It cheers with hope the gloomy day,
>   And sweetens every bitter cup.
>
> It makes the coward spirit brave,
>   And nerves the feeble arm for fight;
> It takes its terror from the grave,
>   And gilds the bed of death with light.
>
> The balm of life, the cure of woe,
>   The measure and the pledge of love,
> The sinner's refuge here below,
>   The angels' theme in heaven above.

Possibly the best conclusion of this attempt to convey the Christian attitude about the Cross will be to quote a prayer widely used by military chaplains for the Blessing of Crosses:

> Bless, O Lord, this image of thy holy Cross, and grant that he who wears it, and all who behold it, may ever remember that the immortal Father so loved us that he spared not thee.

THE CROSS

The great Fathers saw in the account of the Garden of Eden a deeply mystical symbolism in the Tree of Life. As is usual with accounts of deep religious significance, later legends will provide specific details of a very mundane nature—details which were utterly lacking in the original. Thus the later legends of the Cross tell of Seth placing under the dead Adam's tongue three seeds from this Tree. The legend identifies Adam's grave with Golgotha, and later icons show Adam's skull beneath the Cross of Calvary—the Cross itself having grown up from an original seed of the Tree of Life. Later medieval and Renaissance piety tended to confuse this icon and to assume that the skull was a reference to the ever-present fact of death as an individual Christian must face it.

THE CROSS AS AN ANCIENT RELIGIOUS SYMBOL

Ancient cultures abound with examples of crosses used with specifically religious meaning. Egyptian hieroglyphics illustrate at least three types: First, a cross with four square arms, used as a symbol of the four elements, a circle at the crucial point (the intersection) indicating "divine potentiality." The second and best-known form is a T-shaped cross (known technically as a Tau cross), with a circle or loop above it, the whole being a symbol of life. (Heraldry knows this cross under the name of *crux ansata.*) The third form is a long cross, surmounting a figure which looks much like a human heart.

Another form of cross, made up of four arms curving outward, with the outer edges straight (known in heraldry as the *Cross Pattée),* was impressed on the cakes used in certain religious and ceremonial feedings.

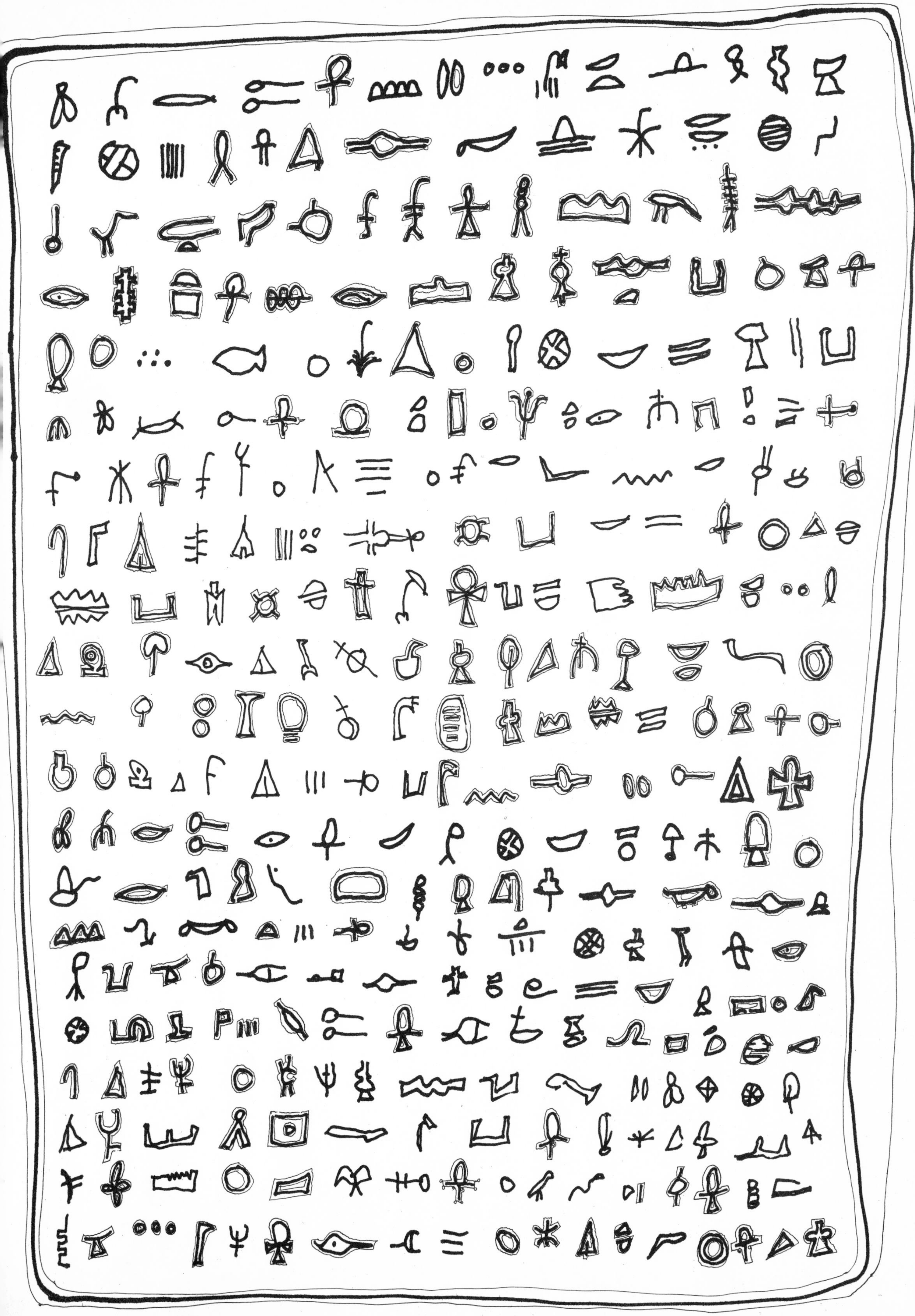

The Egyptian Pharaohs were supposedly descended from the sun god, Ra. Ra, however, is a deity known in trinity, or possibly, more technically, as a triad: Ra, Amon-Ra, and Amon. The second person, Amon-Ra, was the one better understood by the people. He it is who is shown wearing Pharaoh's crown, and holding in his hands the *crux ansata* of eternal life and the scepter of peace. The Egyptians believed that Amon-Ra had both a divine and a human nature, and that it was he who both gave them wisdom and defended them from evil.

The cross as a symbol was equally well known among the Chaldeans, Phoenicians, and Aztecs. The ancient Greeks, the Babylonians, the East Indians, and the Egyptians used the cross and a circle (or arc) as a basic astronomical sign, indicating the planets in this way.

The most interesting is the symbol of the Earth—a complete circle with a cross filling it.

In India, the moving story of Krishna tells of this god-man's crucifixion. Thus the cross is common to Indian religious iconography.

A "voided" cross, with four equal arms, signifies the four rivers, God, the human soul, and nature, instinct with the life generated by this combination.

One of the most ancient forms of cross is the curious one which seems to be made up of four L's. It is the same form as the swastika reversed. This type of cross, so popular for so many years (until its recent perversion), is known under the following names: *gammata*—on the theory that it is made up of four gammas; *croix gammée; fylfot; cross rebated;* and *swastika.*

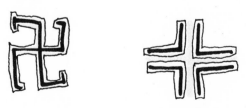

Ancient Assyria developed a majestic form, known as the *feroher*, the principal portion being a winged globe. One famous example from Nineveh shows the deity Ashur, who fights for his people in battle. The whole figure is in the form of a Tau-shaped cross. The greatest authority on the subject says that the most probable conjecture is that "the circle typifies eternity, while the wings express omnipresence, and the human figure symbolizes wisdom or intelligence."(44)

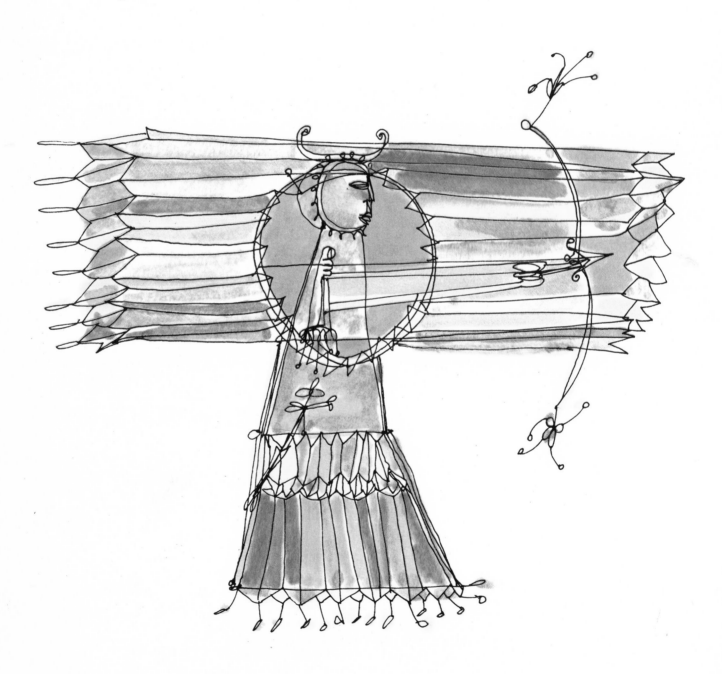

The peoples of Italy, twelve centuries B.C., regularly used crosses to decorate their vessels.

At Villanova the cross was to be found on cinerary urns.

In France, the most ancient coins of the Gauls were marked with a cross.

Inscribed on an ancient chalcedony found in Sicily is the figure of Jupiter holding in one hand the image of victory, and in the other, a double-barred cross.

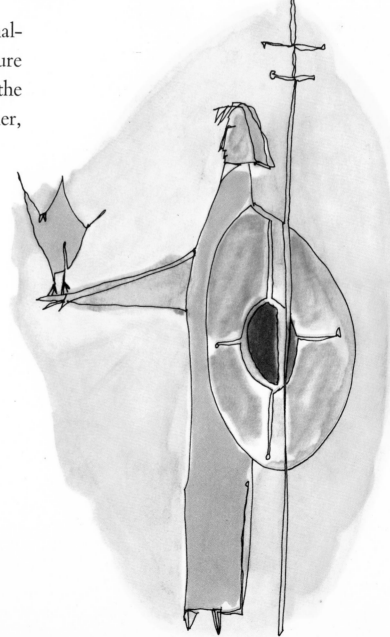

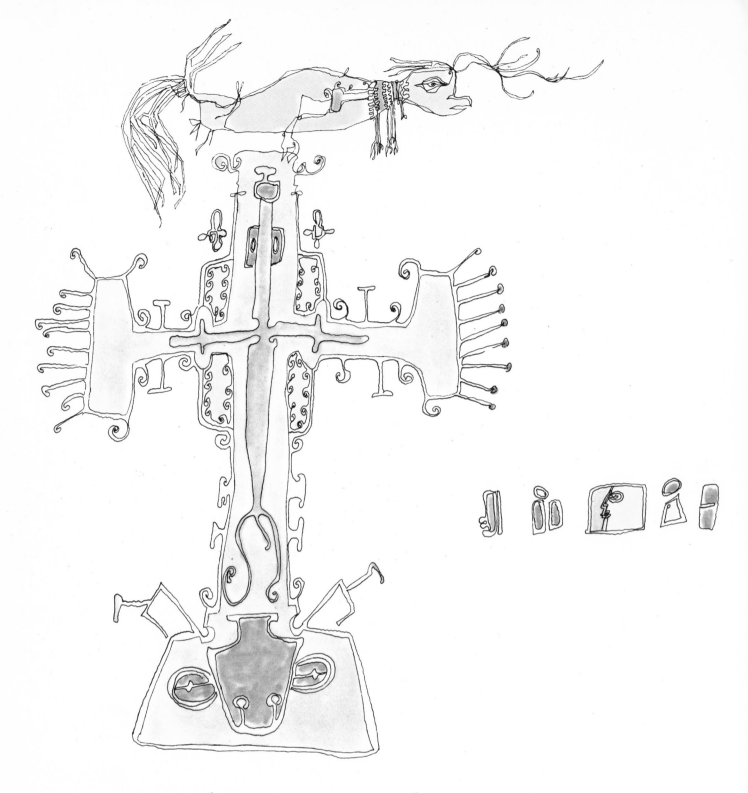

In Palenque, in Mexico, are the remains of an ancient Aztec temple. At the back of one of the altars in that temple is a bas-relief cross some ten feet high. It is a superb design, rich in symbolic carving. Above the cross perches the figure of a bird. The specific meaning of this latter symbol is not known.

These illustrations are but a few examples of the well-nigh universal use of the cross prior to the Christian era, or distinct from a Christian ethos.

THE OLD TESTAMENT "PREFIGURES"

As has been indicated in the Introductory Essay, the typological thinking of the early Fathers was such that they fastened devoutly on any and every Old Testament reference to wood, or to a tree, or a staff, or a rod, or even a stick, seeing in it a prefigure of Christ's Passion. The ancient Church saw in the account of the sacrifice of Isaac a prefigure of Christ's sacrifice. The touching phrase "God will provide himself a lamb" moved the Fathers deeply.

They saw in the picture of Isaac bearing the wood to the mountain for his own sacrifice a direct symbol of Christ.(45) Some even went as far as to insist that Isaac carried the wood in cruciform shape. The important thing, however, was the wood itself. Wood always spoke of a cross.

The one Old Testament passage used universally by the Fathers to press home their point is that which describes Moses making a serpent of brass and placing it upon a pole, so that all who had been bitten by fiery serpents might look upon this symbol and live.*(46)* Tertullian sees it as the "serpent"—the devil—"made a show of" by being hanged from the cross, so that he who gazed on the cross was freed from the bite of the serpents—the devils.*(47)*

Simple and not too easily identified forms of the cross were popular among Christians. The *trident* of the pagan world was in common use. The Egyptian *crux ansata,* the X-shaped cross—in reality the letter Chi—the T-shaped or Tau cross, are all to be seen in early decorations and carvings.

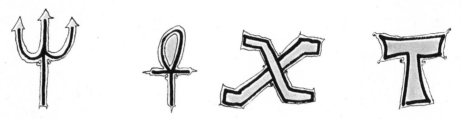

As Panofsky states, in Christian iconography "we study the symbols and their meanings as intended by the artists. ... Iconography is not interested in form, *per se,* but considers the type, searches for origin, and uncovers signification."*(48)*

One of the most ancient symbols devised to represent the cross was the *anchor.* This form of the cross may be seen in some of the most primitive portions of the Catacombs.

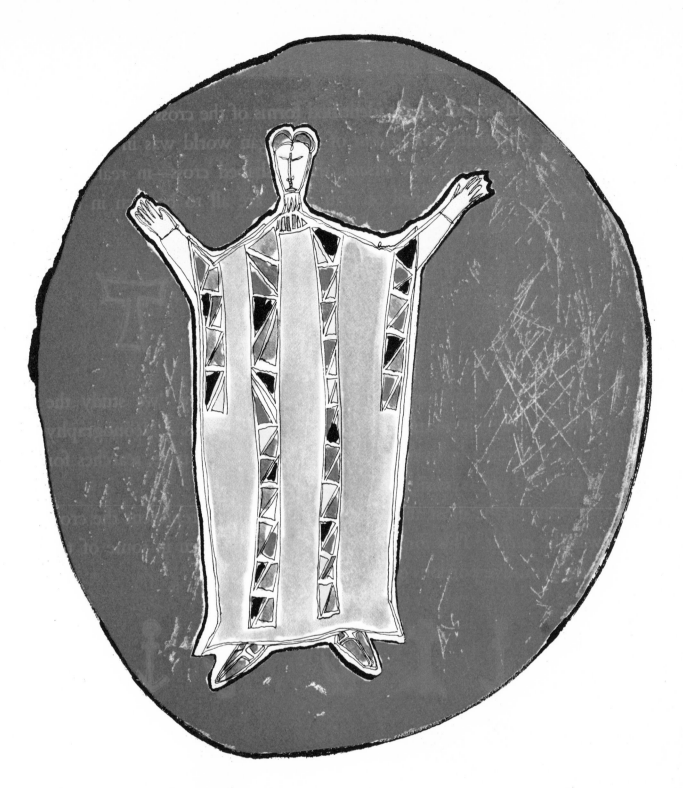

One of the commonest portrayals of a devout Christian in early Christian art is the *orant*. In ancient iconography, Christ was more often than not symbolized by the figure of a youthful shepherd, or as Orpheus; it would only be from the surrounding figures that one could determine whether or not this was intended as a Christian icon. An orant standing and praying in cross-fashion was a sure sign.

Reverence for the person of Christ precluded for the early Church any attempt to show what he looked like. Rather the Church was interested in showing his nature. The Biblical figure for Christ was the Lamb of God. This figure became popular in the fourth century.

Paulinus of Nola, writing about the year 400, says: "Beneath the bloody Cross stands Christ in the form of a snow-white Lamb consigned to unmerciful death."

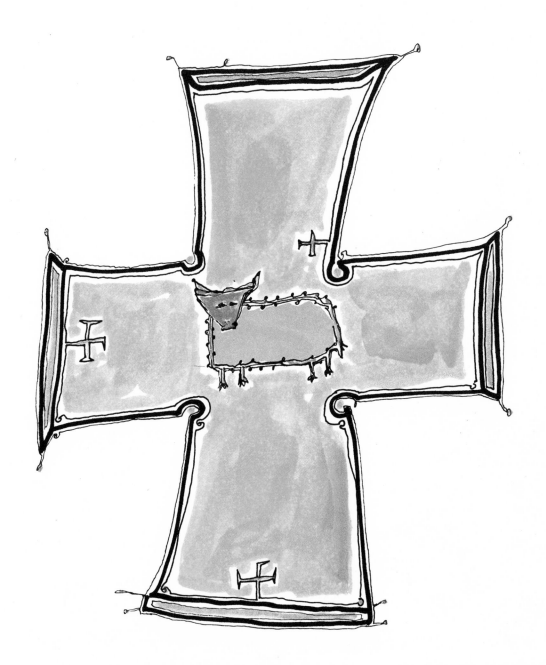

Eventually, the Lamb is placed upon the Cross itself. This is, of course, the remote beginning of the crucifix.

One of the ancient symbols placed upon the Cross was the *Manus Dei*. This, the "Hand of God," derives its title from the eighth chapter of Ezekiel, in the Vulgate Version. When placed upright (this illustration shows the Latin form), it is symbolic of the Blessing of God. When the hand is lowered so that the fingers are down, it symbolizes creation. The Cross shown here is richly adorned.

On the sarcophagi, one sees the Cross beneath the Sacred Monogram. The centuries of persecution had, of course, made Christians extremely timid about disclosing to the world the symbols of their Faith. The two most ancient forms known, apart from the fish (a secret acrostic, which used the first letters of the Greek words for "Jesus Christ, God's Son, Saviour," to produce the word *ichthus,* which means "fish"), are shown in the Chi Rho, treated as a monogram, and the double form of it, which ends by seeming to be a combination of a cross and an X. Note: This latter form is much like the *parahelion* which is customarily assumed to account for Constantine's experience.

The year 312 was marked by Constantine's vision and the setting up of his *Labarum* (standard) with the Sacred Monogram of Christ upon it. As has been noted before, this form of the monogram includes the customary ancient form of the Cross. The version of the *Labarum* shown here is taken from a medal of Constantine.*(49)* The Venerable Bede tells of St. Augustine (of Canterbury) and his forty companions coming into the presence of King Ethelbert, bearing "a silver cross for their banner, and the image of our Lord and Saviour painted on a board."*(50)*

Processional crosses seem first to have been used in the outdoor processions which so helped to popularize Arianism. St. John Chrysostom countered by introducing Orthodox processions of even greater splendor. Within a century after this, processional crosses were in common use. It should be noted that by the ninth century two versions of this cross exist: one, the ordinary type which is used in connection with any religious procession, and, two, a type reserved for use by patriarchs, metropolitans, archbishops (in the West), legates, and sovereigns as a symbol of authority. The scepter-staff of Orthodox bishops and the ancient pastoral staffs of Celtic bishops are forms of the latter type.

The portrayal of Christ on the Cross, an event earlier shown in the purely symbolic figure of a Lamb, begins in the sixth century to be a more literal representation. A human figure is substituted for the Lamb. As yet there is no effort to make Christ's human appearance identifiable save in terms of the symbol of his Passion.

The illustration is of one famous example from a sixth century *Evangeliarium*.

The custom of showing a youth as symbolic of Christ became popular in the fourth century. This figure was gradually adorned with the symbols of his Mission and Triumph.

A figure of the Good Shepherd with nimbus (halo) and cross was used in a tomb built by the Empress Galla Placidia in 440.*(51)*

This particular type of figure ultimately becomes an almost standard representation of the Resurrected Lord.*(52)*

The obvious conclusion of the movement toward identifying the Cross with its Bearer is the crucifix. The decision of the Council in Trullo (692) gave the final blessing to an inevitable process.

The first crucifixes were austere pictures of the Young Man Crucified. The figure, fully clothed, was generally resting against the Cross, rather than attached to it. The attitude was that of One reigning from the Tree.

A famous example of this is the Hohenlohe Siegmaringer Crucifix. It has one curious exception to general practice in that the tunic which Christ wears is not sleeveless. The sleeveless tunic, extending from the neck to the feet, was usual.

Paintings of the crucifixion preserved the purple robe mentioned in *The Gospel of Nicodemus*. The figures of the Blessed Virgin and St. John were introduced; they stood in calm meditation at either side of the Cross.*(53)* (This grouping is technically known as the Holy Rood.)

Occasionally, as on the lid of a box from the Lateran treasure now in the Vatican, the figures of two soldiers are introduced: one (traditionally Longinus) pierces the Lord's side with a spear; the other offers the sponge in response to the cry, "I thirst." One of the most famous examples is an eighth century fresco in Santa Maria Antiqua, Rome.

It is to be noted that the Crown of Thorns was not shown on the head of the Crucified until the tenth century—and then only in the West. The practice did not become general in the West until the thirteenth century.

The enthroned and reigning Christ was, in the East, ordinarily shown with the Blessed Virgin and St. John Baptist standing on either side of him; in the West, more often with the Four Evangelists. The Evangelists might be indicated by books, figures, or by the symbols which had come gradually to be associated with each of them: the angel for St. Matthew, the winged lion for St. Mark, the winged ox for St. Luke, and the eagle for St. John.

Transplanted Byzantine artists gave to Venice a splendid background for free adaptation of the austere theological art of the East. One famous example, now in Bologna, shows Christ about to ascend a ladder to his Cross. It is a remarkable combination of Johannine and Patristic thinking. "The cup which my Father hath given me, shall I not drink it?"*(54)* and, "He [Jacob] said he had seen a ladder, and the Scripture has declared that God stood above it. But that this was not the Father, we have proved from the Scriptures."*(55)*

The first crucifix portraying a dead Christ was in a fresco dating from the eleventh century.*(56)* From this time on, the practice grew in direct proportion to the theological emphasis on Christ's atoning death. Some resistance was encountered. The change from having the feet of the Crucified shown as free, then shown as bound, then shown as nailed, to having them both fastened by one nail was viewed with alarm. The last form mentioned was at first denounced as a heretical innovation of the Albigenses.

The economic and social difficulties of ordinary European men gave a powerful impulse to this portrayal of a Lord who suffered more than they. St. Bernard and St. Francis both left their mark on popular devotion; *Piers Plowman* expressed it in words of the common man. Chaucer can only be understood in the light of this attitude, and Dante is lucid only to those who read him with the knowledge that he combines scholastic theology with popular piety in a work of profound mystical insight.

As life became more difficult and confused, the ancient "mysteries," performed in churches and in processional religious settings, turned into "Passion plays," performed outdoors. The former had been miracle plays expounding sacred subjects; the latter were a great popular identification of human misery with the one greatest Tragedy of all time.

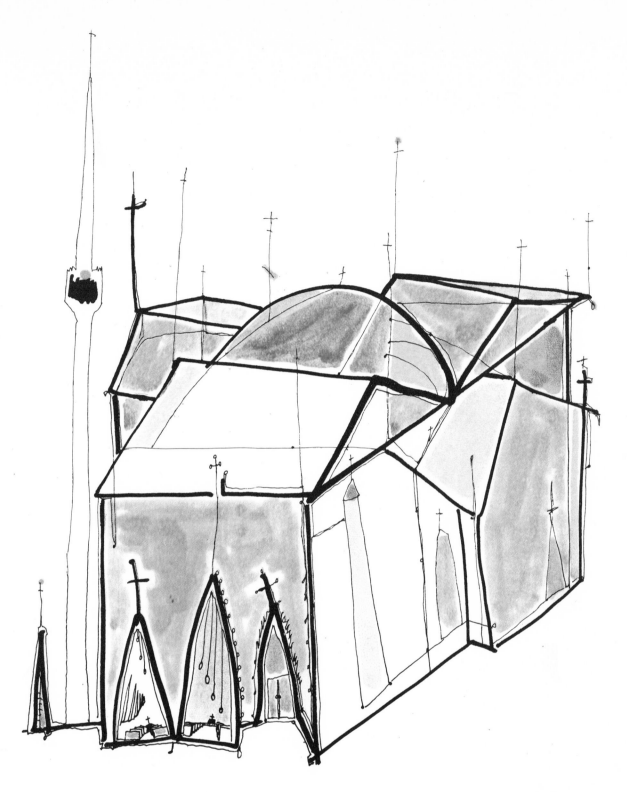

The popularly held notion that churches ought always to be built in a cross-formed (cruciform) shape is derived chiefly from the Victorian Gothic school, which documented its ideas by quoting a famous thirteenth century bishop—William Durandus.*(57)* Their quotation ignored, however, a later sentence which recognized that churches were also to be found in the shape of circles.*(58)*

The cruciform shape was a functional rather than an iconographic conclusion. The Eastern Church largely preferred the so-called "cross-in-square" form; the Western Church, the so-called "basilican" form (shaped like either a Latin cross or a Tau cross). The pure Greek cross form (four equal arms) was relatively rare with a few most noble exceptions:*(59)* the Church of the Holy Apostles, Constantinople (sixth century); St. Mark's, Venice (eleventh century); St. Front, Périgueux (twelfth century); St. Peter's, Rome (sixteenth century); and St. Paul's, London (seventeenth century).

Architects are far more impressed by the functional utility of the "cross-in-square" form than by sentimental arguments about its appropriateness. (This may have a profoundly religious application for preachers to consider.)

Durandus stated that a church was "ornamented within and not without."*(60)* This statement would still have been true of most churches in his own day, for, save the porches, there were few exterior symbols displayed. There is little evidence for the use of crosses on the gables and towers of Western churches much before the eleventh century. Hugh of St. Victor mentions the twelfth century practice of placing the cross above a round ball on top of church towers—but always under weathercocks—and sufficiently open so as not to impede the wind.*(61)* Whether the arms of this cross (generally four) were oriented so that men might tell the direction of the wind is not clear. Few early Gothic churches have crosses integrated into their stone structure. Often, as in Spain and England, the gables were surmounted by architectural forms of floral design. The twelfth century Collegiata of San Isidoro, at León, has only the ball and cock atop its spire.*(62)*

In the seventeenth century, crosses on gables and spires began to be popular. St. Peter's, Rome, and St. Paul's, London, certainly did much to familiarize people with the practice.

Eastern churches, notably Russian ones, have used multitudes of exterior crosses for centuries. Although the Russian Church uses Greek and anchor crosses, the characteristic one is the three-barred variety which derives from formalized Byzantine reverse perspective.*(63)*

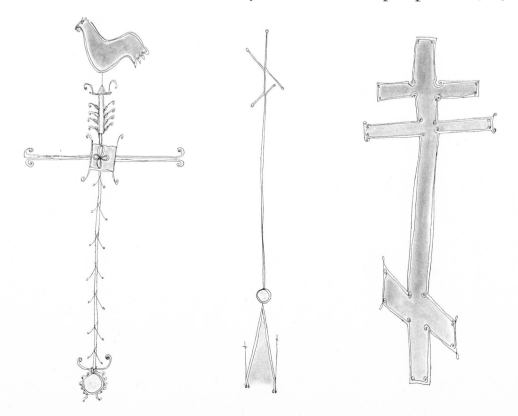

Professor Morey, in a most telling passage, describes the art of the late Gothic period.

"The diabolism of Bosch, the atrocious cruelty in the Passion altarpieces, the cadavers on the tombs reveal a taste that found the evil aspect of experience convincing. It expresses a 'sense of pain' comparable to that of the Hellenistic period which found issue in the agony of the *Laocoön* and the *Flaying of Marsyas*. The cause in both cases was much the same—the collapse of a code of reference; the classic morale was dying in the Hellenistic world and Europe of the fifteenth century was feeling the disintegration of High Gothic faith. . . . The cult of the individual with which the Middle Ages ended was turned by the Renaissance in Italy into an apotheosis of man for which it borrowed the vocabulary of classical antiquity; the North, immersed in reality, clung to the native idiom. The 'grand style' achieved in its final form a divorce of beauty from truth, establishing an academic point of view, whose *a priori* norms and exotic loveliness had no necessary root in experience."

Noting the continuation of the Gothic tradition in Holland, Morey remarks on "the two contributions of late Gothic passed on to modern art—the candid portrait of person and thing, and landscape in its own right, reflective of mood, wherein the modern soul still seeks to recover that communion with the infinite which was the initial and essential content of medieval art."*(64)*

One of the most tragic instances of the angry use of symbols is, from this distance, to be seen in an internal struggle within the Gallican Church in the seventeenth century. One group used the figure of the Crucified with his arms extended horizontally to signify that he died for everyone; the other used the figure with the arms in almost vertical position to indicate that he died for an elect individual. Quite apart from the merits of the arguments involved, the simple fact is that both *symbolic* points of view are true for a Christian.*(65)*

The use of particular types of crosses to identify particular religious groupings was, however, no new idea. Whereas the ancient Church had recognized no exclusive use of one type by either East or West, the schism between them, which became final in 1054, made both hypersensitive to the separate loyalties implied. Henceforth the Greek cross comes to be regarded as indicative of one loyalty, and the Latin cross of a different loyalty.

One famous cross denoting a particular religious loyalty is the Huguenot Cross. It is the Languedoc Cross with the Dove of the Holy Spirit suspended below it.

One ancient form of cross (a Greek one) is associated with letters and a word, dear to the Greek-speaking Christians of early days. The Greek form of Jesus (IHCOYC) and the Greek form of Christ (XPICTOC) were abbreviated into IC and XC and the Greek word for "conquers" (NIKA) was added below the arms. The broken lines above the letters indicate abbreviation.

This splendid design is still stamped upon the Altar bread of the Eastern Orthodox Church. After being cut from the loaf it is referred to as "the Lamb."*(66)*

Particular types of crosses have, since medieval times, come to be associated with individual Feasts and Fasts of the Church Year, and with individual saints—as their personal symbols.

The Passion Cross (or *Cross Urdée*) is pointed at the ends. It is also known as the Cross of Suffering.

When shown rising from out of a chalice it represents the Agony in Gethsemane.

The poignancy of the Passion has caused men to find a variety of ways to express it. The *Cross Portate* speaks of Christ's weary progress to Calvary.

The *Cross Cordée* recalls the ropes with which Christ was bound.

The *Cross Engrailed* reminds men of the sharpness of suffering—the thorniness of pain.

Three crosses behind the rent Veil of the Temple symbolize the hour of Christ's death.

The Crucifixion itself is symbolized by a Greek cross placed between four nails.

The *Calvary Cross* (or the *Graded Cross*) is a Latin cross placed on steps. These steps (or *grieces*) may, technically, vary in number, but the usual number is three.

The *Easter Cross* is a Latin cross with rays emerging from the crucial point. It is also known as the Cross in Glory.

The Ascension is symbolized by the *Cross above the Orb*. It is known as the Cross of Triumph. In imperial and royal regalia it stands as a reminder "that the whole world is subject to the Power and Empire of Christ."*(67)*

The Sermon on the Mount is suggested, in strict symbolism, by the Sacred Monogram above a mountain on the Sea of Galilee.

The saints have, since medieval times, had assigned to them their own heraldic symbols. Many of these originate in the tradition of the particular saint's death.

Thus St. Andrew is known by the *saltire,* an X-shaped cross, which is the legendary form of the cross on which he was crucified. In strict heraldry, *St. Andrew's Cross* is a silver saltire on a blue shield.

St. Patrick's Cross is a red saltire on a silver shield.

St. Alban's Cross is a gold saltire on a blue shield.

St. Osmund's Cross is a black saltire on a gold shield.

A cross of eight points—the *Maltese Cross*—is a symbol of St. John Baptist. It has become famous as the badge of the Order of St. John of Jerusalem (commonly called the Hospitalers). In heraldry it is shown as silver on red, or as silver on black, depending on its use.*(68)*

The Banner of Victory is a pennon of white or gold, charged with a red cross, and displayed from a cross-topped staff. It is assigned variously to symbolize the Resurrection, St. John Baptist, St. James Major, and the Phrygian Sibyl.

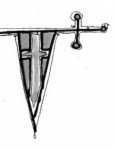

The *Cross of St. George* is a Greek cross terminated by the boundaries of the shield on which it is placed. It is a red cross on a white (or silver) shield.

A gold cross on a purple shield is the *Cross of St. Helena.*

Some crosses have acquired particular association because of their place of origin.

 The *Jerusalem Cross* has become famous as the prime Crusader's symbol. It was on the later form of arms assumed by the Crusader kings of Jerusalem. In ordinary heraldry it is unique in that the cross (a cross *potent* between four crosslets) is gold and yet is placed on a silver shield.

 Another cross which dates from Crusading days is the *Cross Fitchy.* Fitchy means "fixable"—that is, capable of being planted in the ground. It is presumed to derive from the practice of taking oaths on a sword hilt, which, with the blade, formed a cross.

Celtic is a generic title for the types of crosses common to the ancient peoples of Britain, Cornwall, Wales, Ireland, and Scotland. They range in style from crosses carved on the tops of columns (as at Inverary) to crosses carved on monoliths (as on the Isle of Man) to the great standard crosses of Ireland (such as the Drumcliff Cross). The superb cross at Iona is another example of the third type.

Some of these crosses have circles around the crucial point, but it is difficult to determine whether these circles were originally devised for the purpose of giving support to the arms, or for purely symbolic reasons.

The rich incisions and carvings are common to Byzantium and Gaul, but numbers of the existing crosses seem to have received their immediate inspiration through the Vikings and the Danes.*(69)*

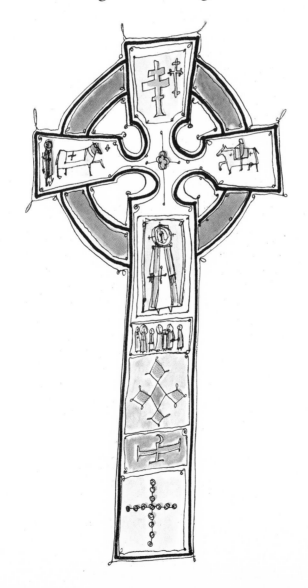

59

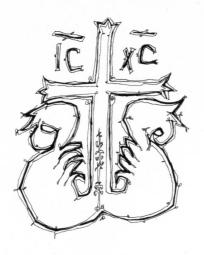

Elaborate Byzantine decoration exploited every possibility of the cross. This superb example from the Church of the Transfiguration at Christianoupolis is characteristic of the East's artistic inventiveness.

The *Cross Cercelé* is a Western heraldic term for one of the Byzantine designs.

Another form popular on Mount Athos is responsible for the Western versions known as the *Cross of Lorraine* or as the *Patriarchal Cross.(70)*

The *Papal Cross* seems to have been developed by artists and heralds in the latter half of the fourteenth century, as in hierarchical distinction to the then recently designated *Patriarchal Cross.* It is by now recognizable throughout the world as a symbol of the Papacy.*(71)*

One form of cross, the *Pall* (or *Forked*) *Cross,* derives its shape from an ecclesiastical vestment—the pallium. In common with the pallium, it symbolizes the "Yoke of Christ" —to be borne with humility.*(72)*

The *Cross Crénelé*, with its suggestion of medieval fortifications, is an obvious symbol of the Church Militant.

The *Cross Crosslet,* made up of four crosses meeting at their bases, is symbolic of Epiphany—the manifestation of Christ to all creation. When placed diagonally (*in saltire*) it is known as the Cross of St. Julian.

The *Cross Cotised* is the name given to a quasi-heraldic form of cross which terminates in scrolls. Its obvious application to the Gospels has made it popular.*(73)*

The arms of the *Cross Flory* end in fleurs-de-lis. It has come to have association with the Blessed Virgin, and therefore stands for the Annunciation.

The *Cross Barby* ends in fish spears. Since the fish was one of the two most ancient symbols of Christ, and the Gospel has numerous religious references to fish and to the Disciples as "fishers of men," this cross is rich in its symbolism.*(74)*

The ends of the *Cross Botonée* terminate in trefoils. Its medieval connection with the Holy Trinity has made its use popular in all decorative forms of printing.

The *Chain Cross* is a medieval heraldic variation of the cross. Its obvious connection with the chains of sin makes this cross a reminder that, from the Christian's point of view, these chains can be broken only by the Cross itself.

The *Cross Ancettée,* technically, has the heads of animals at its terminations. The legendary virtues of particular animals bespeak the virtues to be emulated by the individual wearing the cross.

The *Cross Pattée* (or *Formy*) is probably the most widely used of all heraldic crosses. Victorian piety saw in it a representation of the sheltering wings of a bird, and therefore of "the protecting power of the Cross."*(75)*

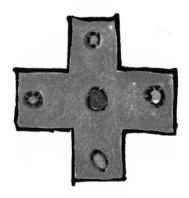

The *Five-Jeweled Cross* has five red stones set in it to signify the wounds of Christ. It brings to mind the address in the English form of an ancient anthem, "O Saviour of the world, who by thy Cross and precious Blood hast redeemed us."

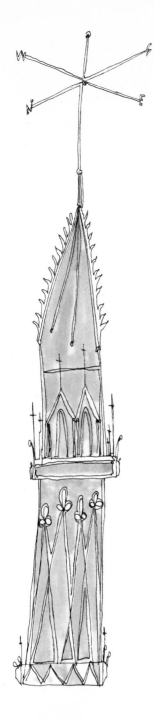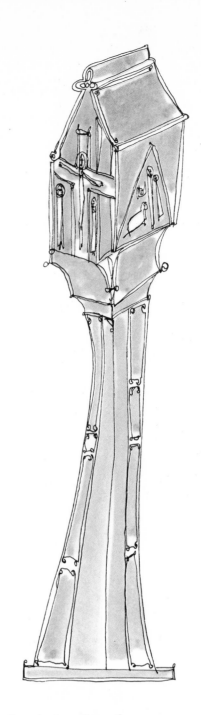

Wayside crosses were popular in the East from the fourth century on. Actually, in those early days, they marked the directions. In medieval days they abounded; they were to be found in market places and at crossroads. They marked the last "resting places" (quite literally) of the great—such as the Eleanor crosses, and noted for all time the grief and lamentations of the suffering.

The first illustration shows the famous Tottenham Cross; and the second, one of the best known examples of a "weeping cross"— *Ampney Crucis,* near Cirencester.

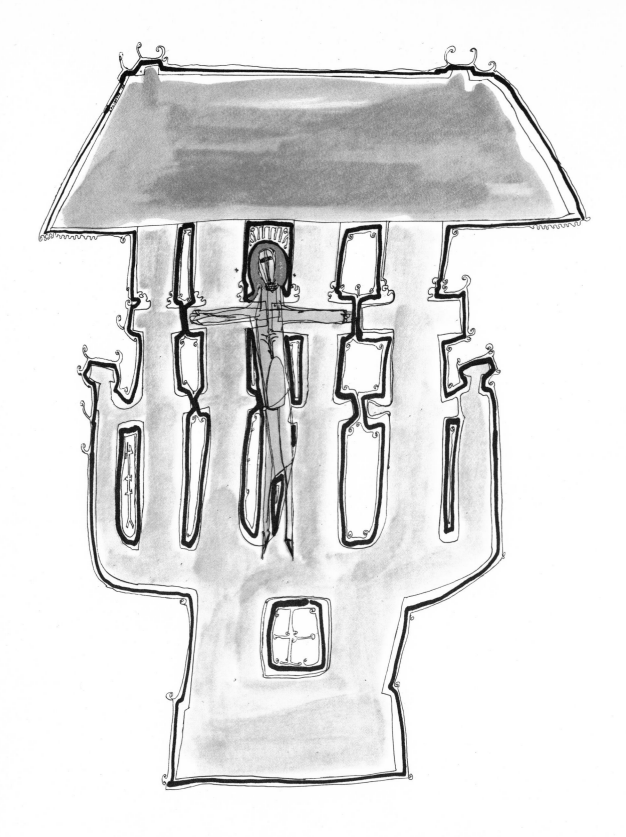

In Romania, where crosses have stood for centuries, there are beautiful ones of a strange form. They are made up of series of crosses, and in silhouette produce the effect of a group of people attendant at the Crucifixion.

We have together examined the Cross as seen through the eyes of the great Fathers, the eyes of saints, and sovereigns, of soldiers and sinners, but we have yet to see its picture in the culture of our own time. There is need, if the symbol be valid, to find its expression in the gears, the electricity, and the very atoms which will, in the future, give power to a world still young as planets go.

Recently, a great physicist managed to take a photograph of the atoms present in a single crystal of metal at the tip of a platinum needle—magnified 750,000 times! It looks like this:(76)

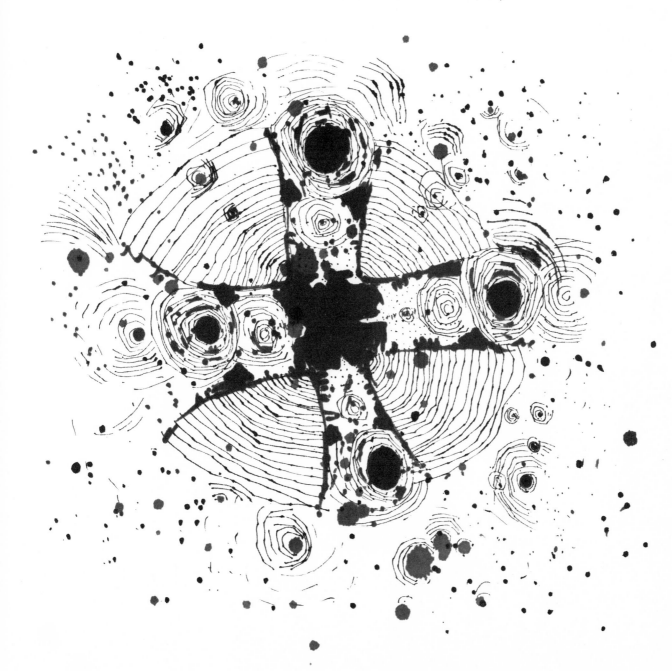

Durandus would have read it as a mystical pre- (or post-) figure, but the great Fathers would have seen in it a newly discovered fellow creature crying out for Baptism, under the saving Sign. New triumphs may yet be added to the symbol to which eight hundred and twenty million human beings own allegiance.

A section of the First Canon from the Orthodox Feast of the Elevation of the Precious Cross seems apposite:

> The Rod is accepted as the symbol of a mystery;
> for by its budding-forth it designated the Priest;
> and in the Church which before was barren, there
> now hath budded forth the Tree of the Cross for
> her power and strengthening.

BIBLIOGRAPHY

Art Bulletin, The, New York, Vol. XXX, 1933, p. 241.

Benson, George Willard. *The Cross—Its History and Symbolism.* Privately printed. Buffalo, 1934.

Bettini, Sergio. *Mosaici Antichi di San Marco a Venezia.* Istituto Italiano d'Arti Grafiche, Bergamo, 1944.

Boutell's *Heraldry,* revised by C. W. Scott-Giles. Frederick Warne & Co., Ltd., New York, 1950.

Brightman, F. E. *The English Rite.* Rivingtons, London, 1915. Two volumes.

Broby-Johansen, R. *Den Danske Billedbibel i Kalkmalerier.* Gyldendalske Boghandel, Copenhagen, 1947.

Clarke, Lowther, and Charles Harris. *Liturgy and Worship.* S.P.C.K., London, 1932 (six reprints).

Coulton, G. G. *Art and the Reformation.* Alfred A. Knopf, New York, 1928.

———. *Medieval Panorama.* The Macmillan Company, New York, 1946.

———. *Five Centuries of Religion.* Cambridge University Press, London (Macmillan, New York), 1923. Three volumes. A fourth volume was printed in 1950.

Demus, Otto. *The Mosaics of Norman Sicily.* Philosophical Library, New York, 1950.

Didron, M. *Manuel d'iconographie Chrétienne—Grecque et Latine.* Imprimerie Royale, Paris, 1845.

Dijon, Musée de, *Saint Bernard et l'art des Cisterciens.* Dijon, 1953.

Dodwell, C. R. *The Canterbury School of Illumination.* Cambridge University Press, 1954.

Duchesne, Mgr. L. *Christian Worship—Its Origin and Evolution.* Translated by M. L. McClure. S.P.C.K., London, 1949.

Durandus. *Rationale Divinorum Officiorum.* Translated by John Mason Neale and Benjamin Webb. T. W. Green, Leeds, 1843.

Fergusson, James. *A History of Architecture in All Countries.* Dodd, Mead and Company, New York, 1885. Two volumes.

Fortescue, Adrian. *The Ceremonies of the Roman Rite Described.* Burns, Oates and Washbourne, Ltd., London, 1934.

Frazer, James George. *The Golden Bough.* The Macmillan Company, New York, 1931.

Gould, Cecil. *An Introduction to Italian Renaissance Painting.* Phaidon Publishers, Inc. (printed in England), New York, 1957.

Hammett, Ralph Warner. *The Romanesque Architecture of Western Europe.* The Architectural Book Publishing Company, New York, 1927.

Henry, Françoise. *Irish Art in the Early Christian Period.* Methuen & Co., Ltd., London, 1947. Second edition.

Henze, Anton, and Theodor Flithaut. *Contemporary Church Art.* Translated by Cecily Hastings, edited by Maurice Lavanoux. Sheed & Ward, New York, 1956.

Kondakov, Nikodim Pavlovich. *The Russian Icon.* Clarendon Press, Oxford, 1927.

Lübke, Wilhelm. *Ecclesiastical Art in Germany During the Middle Ages*. Translated by L. A. Wheatley. Thomas C. Jack, Edinburgh, 1873.

Lundy, John P. *Monumental Christianity*. J. W. Bouton, New York, 1876.

Macalister, R. A. S. *Ecclesiastical Vestments*. Elliott Stock, London, 1896.

Maria Laach (The Abbey of). *Die Betende Kirche*. Sankt Augustinus Verlag, Berlin, 1926.

McClinton, Katharine Morrison. *The Changing Church*. Morehouse-Gorham Co., New York, 1957.

Morey, Charles Rufus. *Mediaeval Art*. W. W. Norton & Company, New York, 1942.

Norris, Herbert. *Church Vestments—Their Origin and Development*. E. P. Dutton & Co., Inc., New York, 1950.

Ouspensky, Leonid, and Wladimir Lossky. *The Meaning of Icons*. Boston Book and Art Shop, Boston, 1952.

Roberts, Alexander, and James Donaldson, editors. *The Ante-Nicene Fathers* (American Reprint of the Edinburgh Edition). Charles Scribner's Sons, New York, 1899. Ten volumes. Indicated in Notes as ANF.

Schaff, Philip, editor. *A Select Library of the Nicene and Post-Nicene Fathers of the Christian Church*. Charles Scribner's Sons, New York, 1902. Fourteen volumes. Indicated in Notes as PNF.

————, and Henry Wace, editors. *A Select Library of the Nicene and Post-Nicene Fathers of the Christian Church*. The Christian Literature Company, New York, 1890. Indicated in Notes as PNF II.

Seymour, William Wood. *The Cross in Tradition, History, and Art*. G. P. Putnam's Sons, New York, 1898.

Skira, Albert, director of collection. *The Great Centuries of Painting—Byzantine Painting*. Editions Albert Skira, Geneva, 1953.

————. *The Great Centuries of Painting—Gothic Painting*. Editions d'art Skira, Geneva, 1954.

Stafford, Thomas Albert. *Christian Symbolism in the Evangelical Churches*. Abingdon-Cokesbury Press, New York, 1942.

Stikas, Eustathios. *L'église byzantine de Christianou*. E. de Boccard, Paris, 1951.

Swiechowski, Zygmunt. *Architektura na Slasku do Połowy XIII Wieku*. Budownictwo i Architektura, Warsaw, 1955.

Twining, Louisa. *Symbols and Emblems of Early and Medieval Christian Art*. Longman, Brown, Green, and Longmans, London, 1852.

van der Elst, Joseph. *The Last Flowering of the Middle Ages*. Doubleday, Doran & Company, Inc., Garden City, 1944.

Victoria and Albert Museum. *100 Masterpieces—Early Christian and Mediaeval*. London, 1930.

von Simson, Otto G. *Sacred Fortress—Byzantine Art and Statecraft in Ravenna*. The University of Chicago Press, Chicago, 1948.

Webber, F. R. *Church Symbolism*. J. H. Jansen, Cleveland, 1938.

Weidle, W. *Les Icônes Byzantines et Russes*. Electa Editrice, Firenze, 1950.

NOTES

1. Galatians 6:14.
2. St. John 12:32.
3. Deuteronomy 6:4–8.
4. *The Book of Divine Prayers and Services of the Catholic Orthodox Church of Christ,* compiled and arranged by the Reverend Seraphim Nassar, published by the Black Shaw Press, New York, 1938, contains in the Appendices the statement that St. Meletius (who was Patriarch of Antioch in 361) established the custom of making the Sign of the Cross, which derived from his great and remote predecessor, St. Ignatius of Antioch. The Sign of the Cross is made in the Eastern Orthodox Church by joining the thumb and the first two fingers and moving them from the forehead to the breast, and then from the right shoulder to the left shoulder. The Western Church makes it in reverse fashion, as far as the cross-wise movement goes, that is to say, from the left shoulder to the right shoulder. It is to be noted that no particular emphasis is laid on joining the fingers, or indeed of using any one of the three mentioned, when this Sign is made by people in the Western Church.
5. *De Corona,* Tertullian, Chapter 3, The Ante-Nicene Fathers, the Christian Literature Company, N.Y., 1890 (an American reprint of the Edinburgh Edition), Vol. III, pp. 94–95.
6. *Hippolytus and His Age,* Bunsen, London, 1852, Vol. III.
7. *Concerning the Statues,* Homily XIX, Section 14, St. John Chrysostom, Nicene and Post-Nicene Fathers, the Christian Literature Company, N.Y., 1889, Vol. IX, p. 470. An *encolpion* was a slender, flat case, generally of metal, designed to be worn around the neck. In modern days, the Eastern Church uses the word to describe any pectoral icon.
8. *Dialogue with Trypho, a Jew,* Justin Martyr, Chapter LXXXVI, ANF, Vol. I, p. 242.
9. *The Octavius,* Minucius Felix, Chapter XXVIII, ANF, Vol. IV, p. 191.
10. *Ad Nationes,* Tertullian, Chapter XII, ANF, Vol. III, pp. 121–122.
11. A good reproduction of this drawing may be found on p. 181 of *The Cross in Tradition, History, and Art,* by the Reverend William Wood Seymour, Putnam's Sons, New York, 1898. Certain scholars have raised objections to the customary explanation of this drawing. They insist that it is a gnostic drawing of the jackal-headed god Anubis.
12. *Apology,* Tertullian, Chapter XVI, ANF, Vol. III, pp. 30–31.
13. *On the Manner in Which the Persecutors Died,* Lactantius, Chapter XLIV, ANF, Vol. VII, p. 318.
14. *The Life of Constantine,* Eusebius (ante 268–340), Chapter XXVIII, The Nicene and Post-Nicene Fathers, Second Series, Vol. I, p. 490.
15. Eusebius' account is in *The Life of Constantine,* Chapters XLIII, XLIV, and XLV, PNF II, Vol. I, pp. 530–531. The other reference is to the *Catechetical Lectures,* Cyril of Jerusalem, Lecture IV, Chapter 10, PNF II, Vol. VII, p. 21.
16. *The Writings of Sulpitius Severus,* Chapter XXXIV, PNF II, Vol. XI, p. 113.
17. *The Ecclesiastical History,* Socrates Scholasticus, Chapter XVII, PNF II, Vol. II, p. 21.

18. *The Ecclesiastical History*, Theodoret, Chapter XVII, PNF II, Vol. III, pp. 54–55.

19. *Christian Worship, Its Origin and Evolution*, Mgr. L. Duchesne, SPCK, London (Fifth Edition), 1949, pp. 274–275, and *Peregrinatio Etheriae (Silviae)*, Section C. The unedifying legend mentioned shortly after this note, is to be found in PNF II, Vol. I, p. 444.

20. *Selected Writings and Letters; On the Baptism of Christ*, St. Gregory of Nyssa, PNF II, Vol. V, pp. 519–520.

21. *Homilies on St. John*, St. John Chrysostom, Homily LXXXV, PNF, Vol. XIV, p. 317.

22. Interesting fifteenth century reproductions of the legendary history of the Cross illustrating the T shape will be found in *Geschiedenis van het heylighe Cruys*, J. Veldener, London, 1863.

23. *Quinisext Council*, Canon LXXXII, PNF II, Vol. XIV, p. 398.

24. *The Gospel of Nicodemus*, Chapter 10 (Greek Form), ANF, Vol. VIII, p. 430.

25. Described in Seymour's *The Cross*, pp. 173–174.

26. Mentioned by G. G. Coulton, as learned from Julius von Schlosser's *Beiträge zur Kunstgeschichte*.

27. Psalm 21, verse 17, in the Vulgate Version; Psalm 22, verse 16, in the King James Version. St. John 20:24–28.

28. See Note 22. An interesting account of action, reaction, and legends of a crucified bearded female saint is to be found in *Medieval Panorama*, G. G. Coulton, The Macmillan Company, N.Y., 1946, pp. 569–570, and Appendix 26 in *Five Centuries of Religion*, Cambridge University Press (Macmillan), 1923, Vol. I, pp. 545–551.

29. See Note 10.

30. See Note 17.

31. An excellent and most moving portrayal of real crucifixion is to be seen on the Rood of Kelham Chapel, at Newark, Nottinghamshire, England.

32. See Note 24.

33. There was, in the eighth and ninth centuries, a determined attempt to do away with all pictorial representations. This movement is described as the Iconoclastic Controversy. The movement was responsible for the destruction of priceless mosaics, but also brought in, almost by way of the vacuum it created, the powerful cultus of the Cross, and is responsible for the use of gold backgrounds in the later mosaics.

34. *Exposition of the Orthodox Faith*, St. John of Damascus (700–755), Chapter XI, PNF II, Vol. IX, pp. 80–81.

35. *Service Book of the Holy Orthodox-Catholic Apostolic Church*, Isabel Florence Hapgood, Association Press, N.Y., 1922, pp. 167 and 169.

36. *The New Roman Missal*, The Reverend F. S. Lasance, Benziger Brothers, N.Y., 1937, pp. 1195–1196. English translation from *The Prayer Book Office*, the Reverend Paul Hartzell, Editor, Morehouse-Gorham Co., N.Y., p. 725.

37. *The New Roman Missal* (Note 36), pp. 487, 490–491. English translation from the *English Missal*, W. Knott and Son, Ltd., London, 1933, pp. 252 and 254. The first stanza is the standard Refrain in the great hymn *Pange lingua gloriosi*, written by Venantius Fortunatus (c. 530–609). The second Latin selection is from his hymn *Vexilla Regis prodeunt*.

38. *The English Rite*, F. Brightman, Rivingtons, London, 1915, Vol. II, p. 834. *The Book of Common Prayer*, The Church Pension Fund, N.Y., 1945, p. 313.

39. This hymn by Girolamo Savonarola, the great Dominican who was killed in 1498, was translated by Lady Jane Francesca Wilde in 1853. It appears in the Common Service Book with Hymnal of the United Lutheran Church in America (1918).

40. Johann Heermann wrote this hymn in 1644. It was based on a Latin Hymn of Bernard of Clairvaux (1091–1153). The translation, by Catherine Winkworth, was made about 1855. It is to be noted that the law requiring a crucifix in all Danish Lutheran Churches, for example, originates at the time of the Reformation.

41. The author of this famous hymn was Isaac Watts (1674–1748). He wrote about six hundred hymns, and many of them are still extremely popular.

42. The author was John Bowring (1792–1872). He was an English Colonial official, knighted in 1854. His deep religious devotion caused him to write this hymn in 1825.

43. The author was Thomas Kelly (1769–1855). This particular hymn was written in 1815.

44. Quoted from *The Five Great Monarchies of the Ancient Eastern World* by George Rawlinson, Vol. II, pp. 3 and 4.

45. Genesis 22:1–14.

46. Numbers 21:4–9.

47. *In Answer to the Jews*, Tertullian, Chapter X, ANF, Vol. III, p. 166. It is to be noted under this heading that the first Apology of Justin Martyr, Chapter LX (ANF, Vol. I, p. 183), states that Plato borrowed his information about the *Chiasma* from Moses. This passage gave rise to the notion that Plato, in the *Timaeus*, had specifically referred to the Second Person of the Trinity as "stamped upon the universe in the form of a cross."

48. *Studies of Iconology*, Erwin Panofsky, Oxford University Press, New York, 1939.

49. This and other invaluable drawings are included in the standard classic of Jacomo Bosio, *La Trionfante e Gloriosa Croce*, published in Rome in 1610. It is a work of objective scholarship rare in that period.

50. From *The Ecclesiastical History of the English Nation*, by the Venerable Bede (673–735), Everyman's Library, J. M. Dent & Sons, Ltd., London, 1935 (sixth reprint), p. 36. There is some possibility the cross and icon were in one piece, as shown in the illustration. If this be not the case, then the icon would have been borne in the arms of a cleric.

51. The Mausoleum of Galla Placidia.

52. A famous example of this is to be seen in *The Descent into Hades* (eleventh century), a mosaic in the Church of Nea Moni, Cheos.

53. It is because of this passage from *The Gospel of Nicodemus* that a legend grew up to the effect that Nicodemus himself had made the original crucifixes known to the medieval Church, just as St. Luke's touching account of the religious experiences of the Blessed Virgin gave rise to the legend that he painted her portrait. He did!—but not in quite the same medium as that which the legend suggests.

54. St. John 18:11.

55. *Dialogue with Trypho*, Justin Martyr, ANF, Vol. I, p. 242.

56. Experts differ slightly on the date: some place it as 1011; others, as of 1059. It is in the Church of St. Urbino in the old outskirts of Rome.

57. Durandus became Bishop of Mende in 1286.

58. *Rationale Divinorum Officiorum*, Durandus, p. 26. The Templar churches were all circular; they were patterned on the Church of the Holy Sepulchre in Jerusalem.

59. The original cruciform shape seems to have been patterned on classic tombs or mausoleums.

60. *Rationale Divinorum Officiorum*, Durandus, p. 34.

61. *Mystical Mirror of the Church*, Hugh of St. Victor (1097–1141).

62. See Hammett, *The Romanesque Architecture of Western Europe*, for pictures of churches in this period.

63. The gradual development of the Russian cross may be followed by examining the Cross of Lothario in San Clemente, Rome, then an icon of St. Demetrius (Weidle, Plate XXXI), and, finally, an icon of The Descent from the Cross (Kondakov, Plate XXXIX).

64. *Medieval Art*, Charles Rufus Morey, pp. 391–392.

65. For both points of view in this tragic matter see *The Reluctant Abbess*, Margaret Trouncer, Sheed & Ward, Inc., New York, 1957, and *Memoirs of Louis XIV and the Regency*, the Duke of Saint-Simon, George Allen & Unwin, Ltd., London, 1888 (seven reprints), three volumes.

66. It is to be noted that only the portions cut from the loaf are consecrated. The remainder of the loaf is cut into small pieces and, at the conclusion of the Service, is distributed to the congregation. Apart from the "Lamb" cut from the principal loaf, the Russians use small individual loaves for the additional particles to be consecrated.

67. From the English Coronation Service—the *Liber Regalis*.

68. Romantic nineteenth century heraldry saw this cross as composed of four spearheads, and found the eight points symbolic of the Beatitudes.

69. The finest examples date from the late eighth through to the tenth centuries. It will be remembered that Dublin became important as a city only when the Danes invaded Ireland in the ninth century. It continued a Danish city until the Anglo-Normans drove them out in 1170.

70. The Hospitalers had used this form of cross on a staff in the twelfth century.

71. It has been suggested that French heralds were responsible for this distinction. The far more conservative Italian artists were still showing the great and sainted Popes holding the ancient form of cross-staff (an archbishop's) in pictures painted as late as the end of the fifteenth century. (See a painting attributed to B. Conti, in the Pinacoteca di Brera, Milan.)

72. The Y-shaped pallium proper is shown as white, edged with gold, and charged with black *Crosses Fitchy*. It appears, along with the ancient form of archbishops' cross-staff, in the Arms of Canterbury and in the Arms of Westminster.

73. *"Cotised"* does not, in strict heraldry, mean a "scrolled" terminus.

74. See page 36 of this text.

75. Seymour, *The Cross in Tradition, History, and Art*, p. 368.

76. Dr. Erwin W. Müller, Pennsylvania State University. The picture was reproduced in the September, 1958, issue of the *National Geographic Magazine* (Vol. CXIV, No. 3).